religion:
who needs it?

religion:
who needs it?

richard a. seymour
integrity press : lagrange, wyoming

RELIGION: WHO NEEDS IT?
published by Integrity Press

ISBN 978-0-8024-7191-8

Printed in the United States of America

For information:
INTEGRITY PRESS
PO BOX 10
LAGRANGE, WY 82221

Dedicated to the memory of my dad, who saw through so many of the religious games people play.

contents

why religion annoys so many people
chapter one

This book is for all who are irritated by religion. If you've become weary of all the sham and unreality of much that is labeled "religious," if you're disgusted with hypocrites and those you consider to be self-righteous prudes, if the mysteriousness of religion just seems to be one grand fantasy world to you, then this book is definitely for you.

No doubt there are many valid reasons for you to be annoyed, and I'd like to talk with you about some of them because, you see, for a good part of my life I've been bothered by religion too. In some ways, quite a few of the things I see going on even now under the guise of religion really irk me. But ever since I discovered what the Bible is really all about, I've realized that there's a reality that no close-minded person, religious or not, could ever know or appreciate. I found out that merely being religious or nonreligious is not even the issue.

No matter what "brand name" one may go by, it seems that neither religion nor philosophy is adequate to meet the deepest needs of man's nature. For instance, though religions claim varying degrees of insight into major areas that concern man (e.g., the meaning of life, knowledge of God, personal salvation, how to face death, immortality, etc.), they so often only help to ease man's surface symptoms.

If it is true that man is in need of salvation, that he is separated from God, that there is a hell to shun and a heaven to gain, then I can see why some would think that merely to "get religion" is like applying a small bandage to an amputated limb. Something far more adequate than mere religion is needed. On the other hand, it is reasonable to assume that if man doesn't need saving, if there is no God, or if we'll all end up in the same condition anyway, then who needs religion at all?

Unfortunately, it seems that so many in our world have been spiritually drugged into a sort of nebulous, religious way of thinking that leaves them incapable of being truly objective. It's so extreme in some cases that W. T. Stace, longtime professor of philosophy at Princeton University, defined religion as "the hunger of the soul for the impossible, the unattainable, the inconceivable."[1] Regardless of whether you agree with Stace's definition, it's no wonder people become confused, despondent, bitter, or indifferent about the whole thing.

It seems as if everyone claims an inside track to the truth (and we both know they can't all be right), and so many groups seem to think they are God's gift to mankind. At one time or another you have probably felt caught in the middle of the whole mess.

If there's one word to describe why religion annoys so many people, I think it would be the word confusion. When an honest and sincere person begins to investigate the world's religions, with all their claims and counter claims to truth, often the end result is that the seeker either winds up being confused himself or concludes that all the religions are confused.

I've taught religious courses on the college level for more than thirty years, and I sadly admit that I've seen many people become spiritually and emotionally broken, and even suicidal, often due to religious teachings or pressures to conform to an impossible religious mold. Through the past fifty-plus years of my life I've encountered many who at one time attended church regularly, but when I met them they were either indifferent or antagonistic toward church. At first it puzzled me until I began to take a new and really hard look at the whole religious picture. What I saw made me appreciate the difficulty the average non-religious person has in his attempt to decipher spiritual truth from spiritual error. Hopefully this book will be an aid in that attempt.

Fortunately, there is a way out of religious mazes. There is a way to know God and to be sure of going to heaven. You may have confidence that there is a lasting meaning to life, that you have a purpose for being here, and that you are important to God and the world. But being blindly religious is not how to have it—not at all. In fact, the happiest day of my life was when I lost my "religion" and found something far more lasting and satisfying. However, that's another story. For now let's talk about the games religious people play.

notes

1. Quoted in Eugene E. Brussell, ed., *Quotable Definitions* (Englewood Cliffs, NJ: Prentice-Hall, 1970). p. 490.

the games religious people play
chapter two

Here are some of the more common criticisms
that are hurled indiscriminately at religion in
general and at Christianity in particular. Much
is valid in these criticisms; then again, much is
superficial. I feel that I thoroughly understand
both sides of these criticisms, having been
turned off by the whole religious picture for
so long and then discovering what I believe to
be the real truth about the matter. Even now
religion that is false, religion that is bigoted
or greedy, grates on me terribly. But I'm so
thankful that there is truth that can set one free
both from the shackles of the dogmatic religions
of man and from the hopelessness of blind
unbelief.

Here, then, are some things that annoy people
about religion. You're not alone if the same
things bother you; they bother sincere people
the world over. It isn't only the flaws of so-called
Christians that irritate others. I've known
Hindus, Bhuddists, Muslims, and cultists of
various stripes that have been equally bothered
by inconsistencies in their own religious beliefs
and practices. Religion, at best, can be quite
disturbing. Just try to be as honest and open-

minded about the shortcomings of religions as you would want someone to be toward you or your beliefs.

the contradiction of religion
truth, truth, who's got the truth?

"Within Christianity alone are hundreds of denominations and sects, with dozens more cropping up every year, to say nothing of the other world religions, with all their divisions. With so many denominations and religions, how can anyone know which is right, or if any are? Not only are there disagreements between denominations, but often major differences exist within churches and groups. How is it possible to know which one to believe or which ones to take seriously, if any?"

One thing is fairly certain—any religion or church that has a lot of man's opinions woven into its doctrine and practices is, at best, on very shaky ground, a foundation of human opinion. Perhaps the reason there are so many churches and denominations is that man himself is such a contradictory creature.

Of course, man doesn't usually like to admit that he's wrong or being contradictory. As much as he likes to think he's intellectual, he is actually very emotional. Though a man may sincerely believe in something religious, though he may feel it is right, though he may consider his belief to be clean and holy; if that belief originates in man, then it comes from within a creature whose very nature is fickle, and therefore, deceitful and unreliable.

It really shouldn't be any more difficult for a religious person than for anyone else to admit being in error. For instance, many times people "just know" they are in love and that this is the girl or guy for them, or some "just know" that a certain investment will be the one that will finally put them on "easy street." Often such people are lucky to escape with their skin. Then along comes the religious person who has had an experience and "just knows" that he now has a direct hot line to the Creator of the universe.

Of course, there are many differences among religions because the men who create them are all so different. The fact that you are able to detect some of the contradictions among religions indicates that you may have a great deal of good, honest insight. If that's so, my hat is off to you. On the other hand, be careful that your awareness of certain religious contradictions doesn't spring from your own feeling of intellectual or philosophical superiority, which loves to find faults in the people and systems with which you disagree. Also, remember that every person, group, or system probably has something good in it. If you see *only* the negatives in religion, perhaps your own powers of observation are not quite as objective and honest as they could be.

Don't get me wrong. There's probably much in religious circles that's worthy of condemnation. I'm just saying, don't be guilty of one of the very same traits you might condemn in a religious person—close-minded prejudice. That approach is never a help in finding truth for yourself.

the inconsistencies of religion
do as i say, not as i do

It seems to me that too many who regularly attend church don't practice what they preach. They act pious in church on Sunday, and live like the devil the rest of the week.

I'm perfectly aware that some who attend church regularly do not live as Christians should. There is no defense for such conduct. Churches today have their share of hypocrites just as Judaism had its share of them in Christ's time, and He didn't hesitate to label hypocrites for what they were.

It's always true, isn't it, that what we do speaks louder than what we say? It's reputed that Mahatma Gandhi once said he would be happy to become a Christian if he ever saw a real Christian. He was implying that Christians are supposed to be Christlike; and since he had never seen any Christians who were Christlike in their attitudes and actions, he wasn't ready to become a Christian himself.

Of course, people who have only religion can so easily go through the motions of playing a little game called "church." They attend services every week, sing the hymns, follow along in their Bibles as the pastor reads, and sit through the service with a sanctimonious look on their faces, while all the time they're full of bitterness, hatred, bigotry, lust, and all kinds of self-centered yearnings and desires.

The reality of their "faith" comes through loud and clear when they go home. I'm aware that it isn't uncommon for a man or woman to hold an important position in a church, maintaining all the pious outward appearances of religiosity, and yet at home let all the bars down and be as pagan as anyone else. No wonder kids are turned off by the whole religious mess. They see quite clearly that religious beliefs have not really brought any meaningful reality to mom or dad's lifestyle so why should they waste any more of their time on it?

But while all the above is true, aren't there bound to be people in churches who are consistent? What about them? If the hypocritical ones prove something, what do those who are honest and sincere prove? Might they not prove that there is a reality in their lives that is genuine? I've known some coaches, businessmen, and parents whom I felt couldn't be trusted any farther than I could throw an elephant, but that hasn't caused me to flatly condemn all coaches, businessmen, and parents.

I guess the watchword should be caution. While picking out the faults and inconsistencies of

others whom you consider hypocritical, you don't
want to be guilty of flatly condemning everyone,
either in the religious world or elsewhere.

the unreasonableness of religion
don't confuse me with the facts, my mind is made up

*I've never gotten used to the way man can be very
logical and scientific in every area of his life until it
comes to his religious beliefs; then he seems to commit
a kind of intellectual and spiritual suicide.*

It is strangely true that in religious issues (as
well as in other areas involving the emotions)
people sometimes will believe whatever they
want to believe, even if contrary to reason. Let's
say someone asks you why you believe the earth
is round. You give them all the astronomical,
mathematical, and scientific reasons at your
disposal and overwhelm them with irrefutable
evidence. Then, imagine further, that they
turn to me and ask me why I think the earth
is round. Suppose my reply is, "Because my
Mommy told me it is; that's why." Would my
illogical reply mean that the roundness of the
earth was a farce? No, not at all. My logic may

be silly, which could lead to some horribly wrong conclusions, but what I believe may still be right.

People believe in many religious fantasies and myths that have no basis in fact. Yet, these same people may believe some things that are absolutely true. It's to your credit if you can see through the fallacious logic of others, but you should be careful, while rejecting their lack of logic, that you don't deny or overlook some kernel of truth that some of them may possess.

I feel certain that the most critical thinking unbeliever could believe in even the miraculous if it could be demonstrated that there is a factual basis for it or that there really is a God who actually does intervene in men's lives. Just as surely, no discerning unbeliever would accept something as astounding as the miraculous simply on the basis of his feelings. That's all right. I believe there's nothing at all wrong with that approach to truth.

There seems to be a kind of institutional mentality[1] that permeates much of the religious world. Perhaps you even have had friends who refused to answer any questions about their religious beliefs, or even to discuss them. That kind of attitude is always sad, because when one is close-minded nothing fresh is ever allowed entrance. Such people eventually become emotionally, intellectually, or spiritually dry. I don't ever want that to happen to me, and I'm sure you don't either.

Nothing frustrates me more, and perhaps you've encountered it too, than to try to discuss religion reasonably with someone who pushes reason aside. It is because of this apparent inability (or unwillingness) to give factual evidence for the validity of their beliefs that has turned so many people completely away from anything religious. Thankfully, though, it is possible to have factually-based beliefs. More about that later.

the fanaticism of religion
the end is near!

I don't appreciate the religious do-gooders who virtually attack people on the streets just to cram their religion down their throats.

I remember reading about Dr. R. A. Torrey,

one of the better-known evangelists and Bible teachers during the early part of the 20th century. Dr. Torrey was walking down a street in Los Angeles when a religious zealot accosted him and, grabbing him by the lapel, asked, "Sir, are you saved?"

Torrey's reply was, "Yes. Thank God!"

Later, in relating the incident, Dr. Torrey expressed the feeling that that kind of person would certainly not have won him to his way of thinking by such a crude, overbearing approach.

Unfortunately, the world is full of unthinking zealots who do more harm than good. However, they are in all walks of life, not just in religions. The overanxious, hard sell salesman; the obnoxious, power hungry politician; and the pushy, money-worshiping businessman are all examples of misguided, fanatical, and repulsive zealots. Yet we don't stop buying from, voting for, or doing business with those people just because our sense of refinement has been offended by such aggressiveness, do we? No, we learn to sift the good from the bad. That's the intelligent way, and it should be our approach to religious beliefs and practices as well.

the strictness of religion
the straightjacket game

It seems to me that the most drab, unhappy people I know are the ones who are the most religious. They seem to have no sense of humor and little appreciation of the finer things of life, and they are always looking at the morbid side of things. I just don't think religion has much of anything to offer.

It does seem sometimes that all the enjoyable things of life are forbidden by some religion, doesn't it? This is what leads so many people to conclude that they won't be ready for church until they have one foot in the grave and the other foot on a banana peel! Then it won't matter too much how strict church is because they'll be ready to settle down and behave anyway.

Religions that convey that the way to heaven or acceptance with God is through some impossible or nearly impossible set of rules remind me of the story of the wild-living, freewheeling bachelor. This guy was only 25 years old, but, because of his unrestrained lifestyle, he looked 50. He went to the doctor for a checkup. The doctor gave him a complete physical examination and found him in good health for a man of 50; but when the bachelor told the doctor that he was only 25, the doctor was shocked. As he asked the bachelor more and more personal questions, he realized the source of his aged appearance. Finally, the doctor told him, "Look, you've either got to change your lifestyle and cut out some of the things you've been doing, or you'll be dead in five years."

This really bothered the bachelor, because he had been having such a great time that he just couldn't imagine giving up so many of the things he enjoyed. Finally, the doctor gave him the ultimatum in unmistakable words: "Keep living as you are and be dead in five years, or cut out your bad habits and live a normal lifetime."

After much mental anguish the bachelor finally decided he'd better change his lifestyle. The first day he cut out drinking, the second day he cut out smoking, the third day he cut out cursing, the fourth day he cut out women, and the fifth day he cut out paper dolls!

Churches and religions that are always negative
are like that bachelor, taking away everything a
person enjoys or that has meaning to him; and
they leave him in a spiritual vacuum. Such an
approach can land a person in a mental ward
"cutting out paper dolls."

It's amazing though, that the Bible does nothing
like that. Jesus promised joy unspeakable,
everlasting life in heaven, and abundant life
here and now (John 15:11, 3:16, 10:10). That
hardly sounds morbid, does it?

Fortunately, there are people and churches
that teach the Bible the way it is, separating
the beauty of scriptural truth from the sham
of man-made religious error. It might just be
worth the effort to search for such a group.

the exclusiveness of religion
do it our way

*Off the top of my head, I can think of five Christian
churches that claim to be the true church of Jesus
Christ. Each one claims to be Christian, and each
claims the Bible as its authority (more or less) though
each interprets the Bible differently. Yet each swears to*

*have an exclusive and an infallible insight into what
the Bible really means, and to be the one and only true
way to God. One thing is certain—they can't all be
right, but they could all be wrong!*

I don't think it would bother you nearly as
much if religious groups would say, "God is
always right, but we're sometimes wrong, so
we'd better find out what God says and follow
Him." Unfortunately, that's not always the way
it seems to be, is it? Sometimes groups like
these will say that God is the One who is always
right, but as you listen to them and read their
literature you can't help concluding that what
they are really saying is that their *interpretation*
of God is what is right. This, understandably,
turns thinking people off immediately.

This exclusive, "private club" attitude bothers
many fine people. In the past this same attitude
has led to horrible persecutions, murders, and
even so-called holy wars—all in the name of God
and truth. But again, we shouldn't be too hasty
in judging God by the imperfections of those who
claim to be His representatives on planet earth,
any more than we should base our sole estimate
of a country upon the lives and characters of its

ambassadors. There are good ambassadors and there are bad ones. There are good churches and there are bad ones.

the mystery of religion
only God knows for sure

There seems to be so much hocus-pocus in religion. You attend the services of some churches, and they go through all kinds of rituals and routines without ever explaining to the visitors what's going on. You go into such services feeling a little bit lost and bewildered about the whole thing, and you come away feeling the same way, or even worse. How's a person supposed to know what's going on, anyway?

I realize that the whole subject of God has an element of mystery. I suppose that's how it should be. However, if there is a God, it seems He would be intent on communicating with His creation and He would remove much of the mystery. Groups that make the idea of knowing or being close to God a vague, mystical experience just push people further from anything to do with God. Often common people just feel that they don't want religion or need it. I can't really blame them much. Too many people just can't relate to religion at all, mostly because of the deep mystery that clouds the whole picture.

Does it really have to be that way? Do we have to go around in a spiritual and intellectual fog all of our lives, wondering where God is (if there is a God), what He is like, and whether we can ever know Him in a meaningful way? I don't think we do at all, and I've got good reasons for thinking that way. I'll share those reasons with you shortly, but for now, let's consider the fantasy of religion.

the fantasy of religion
pretending does not make it so

"Religious doctrines...are all illusions; they do not admit of proof, and no one can be compelled to consider them as true or to believe in them."
-Sigmund Freud, *The Future of an Illusion*

"Religion is the opium of the people. Religion is a kind of spiritual intoxicant, in which the slaves of capital drown their humanity and their desires for some sort of decent human existence."
-Lenin, *Religion*

It finally hit me one day that a great number
of people in this world will believe virtually
anything, even with little or no real reason
for doing so. It seemed that religions often
encourage this type of make-believism,
sometimes to a rather sickening degree.

Then I began to realize that living in a fantasy
world was not the exclusive practice of some
blindly religious fanatics. The two men quoted
at the beginning of this section are good
examples of what I mean. Freud called religious
doctrines "illusions;" but can we honestly believe
that Freudian psychiatry represents the epitome
of factual, real knowledge, when for years the
percentage of suicides has been higher among
psychiatrists than among people of any other
profession? Not only that, but more and more
psychiatrists are admitting that the majority
of the "cured" cases among the mentally ill
would have been cured without the assistance of
psychiatric help.

What of Lenin and other equally devout
atheistic Communists? Would the most
instructed and militant Communist really
expect me to believe that he has not been

"intoxicated" to believe in a future Marxist utopia, "some sort of decent human existence?"

It is most definitely true that religion often has its share of fantasy woven into its fiber, but religion is by no means alone in having that flaw. Though we may feel that we must reject some things we hear about God as being pure fantasy, we should probably also recognize that there is truth about Him that we should not refuse. Also, just because some religious people seem to live in a fantasy world doesn't mean that all who believe in God or the Bible are that way. One can play the game of make-believe in any field: business, politics, sports, or religion, to name just a few. The honest seeker of truth must go deeper than superficially brushing aside all religion as mere make-believe. A more careful examination of the facts is demanded if we are to know real reasons for our beliefs or unbelief.

Perhaps you are one of the growing number of people who see how willing some religious people are to believe what they want to believe with little or no foundation, and so you have simply turned away in pity or disgust. I understand those feelings. You can't understand how otherwise intelligent people can believe such things with no evidence or proof. You recognize that this is one of the grave weaknesses of much that goes by the name of religion—the tendency to live in a make-believe world of fantasy where facts are ignored and where feelings reign supreme.

It's good that you do recognize that, but remember that even those who are nonreligious are often just as gullible, just as capable of believing in their own privately concocted fairy tales as the most religiously inclined person. Try to keep from having what I call a "pigeonhole brain"—classifying people in general categories without thoroughly weighing each person, group, or situation individually.

the greediness of religion
give God the credit, send us the cash

Everywhere you look in religious circles it seems somebody has their hand out for money—from pew rentals, pledges for building funds, to high pressured offerings—it really gets overbearing and sometimes downright disgusting.

I suppose one of the most common criticisms of religion is that churches seem to be always harping on money. For instance, Madalyn Murray O'Hair, who was considered America's best-known atheist during her lifetime, sternly criticized the privilege that churches enjoy in being tax-exempt as nonprofit organizations. Her reasoning went something like this: If churches can own real estate, own motels, and even invest in stocks and girdle factories, then why shouldn't they be taxed? They are as much a profit-making business as any other business.

That's not necessarily bad logic, but not all churches misuse their tax-exempt status any more than all hospitals misuse funds, though we've heard of some that do. Should we, therefore, close down all hospitals? Obviously we shouldn't.

Whether or not you believe churches should be taxed, it is unfortunately true that some churches do seem to dwell heavily upon money. In fact, it became so prevalent in one church that the head deacon said to his wife, "I think our minister's favorite passage of Scripture is 'The Sermon on the Amount!'"

The other side of the story is that more and
more pastors are realizing how this emphasis
on money is turning away many people.
Churches, too, are beginning to play down the
offering. Some have even stopped taking public
offerings altogether; they simply have a box in
which people may place gifts, if they choose. Of
course, those churches that do harp on money
in an overbearing way should be ashamed, and
probably deserve any criticism they get.

the bigotry of religion
i love the world, it's just people i can't stand

*The one institution that should have paved the way for
recognizing all men as equals is the church, but many
churches have dragged their feet miserably in this
area. Now, after riots, revolutions, and Constitutional
amendments, many churches are beginning ever so
grudgingly to join the battle cry for racial equality.
Some church historian of the future will probably
write that the church spearheaded the fight for
equality in our country. Not likely!*

I, too, wonder how different history would be
if all the Christians who came to this country
had helped the Native Americans, and later the

black slaves, as they should have. Thank God, some did; but many did not. Perhaps if they had, we wouldn't be having nearly the problems we now have.

The church is not the only institution or group guilty of bigotry, by any means, but in one sense it should not be guilty of it at all. Nevertheless, as long as churches and religions are made up of people, there will be prejudices, just as there will be predjudices in other groups comprised of humans. In contrast, when Christ was on earth He encountered all kinds of people, yet He showed genuine love and acceptance for all of them. When He walked the hills of Palestine, the Gentiles were often considered no better than mere dogs, not fit for God to love or to save. At the same time, when Christ came upon the scene He showed some of these self-righteous (and often religious) people what they were—hypocrites—and He had compassion on the common man, Jew and Gentile alike.

Some groups that traditionally have been guilty of racial prejudice are now giving the appearance of accepting those of different races and nationalities, but in some cases this may

be no more than the "some of my best friends
are _____" syndrome all over again. There's
a vast difference between tolerance and real
acceptance, and every man should be accepted
for who he is. If God has made every man, then
certainly He has a place for each one and loves
them equally.

Another kind of bigotry also has come to my
attention—the prejudice against those who are
economically and educationally deprived. It has
been pointed out that too often those who are
poor are only tolerated, and they feel completely
inadequate and unworthy around the average
church congregation. Some poor people
apparently feel that they can't go to church
because they don't have nice enough clothes
to wear. This "Sunday go to meetin' clothes"
concept has become an abomination by making
many feel that they're not worthy to worship
in the house of God unless they are "properly"
dressed, but the Bible does not convey such
ideas at all; they are strictly the result of man's
tradition. I know of any number of churches that
would welcome a man in his work clothes, and
that is only as it should be. If I believed I had to
be dressed up to be accepted by God, I think I'd

either find another God or another belief.

I do not want to close this chapter having you think that I approve or condone the abuses and misuses of religions and churches, because I decidedly do not. In fact, I'm not too sure that the last two thousand years of progress in religion have really gotten us any further ahead of where Christ and the apostles were when Christianity began. However, to put a blanket of condemnation over everything religious or "churchy" may not be the best approach either.

If you feel that religion just doesn't cut it, I can understand that; but if it doesn't, what then? What do we do now? Where do we turn? Where do we look for truth or meaning to life? Let's consider some alternatives.

notes

1. A frame of mind that accepts without question what one's leaders proclaim, as when a religionist accepts unquestioningly what a pastor, a priest, a rabbi, or church leader may teach.

where do we go from here?
chapter three

If you are a seeker and lover of truth,
and religion bothers you to the point that
it completely frustrates you, there are
alternatives. But any alternative upon which
you build your lifestyle, and upon which
you establish meaningful priorities and
standards, would be some kind of philosophy.
By "philosophy" I mean what Charles W. Eliot
defined as "the thoughts of men about human
thinking, reasoning and imagining, and the
real values in human existence." You'll end up
either adopting someone else's philosophy as
your own, or adapting another's philosophy to
fit some ideas that you already have, or simply
creating your own philosophy. In any case,
your alternative to religion will be some sort of
philosophy.

Philosophies, like religions, are not without
problems of their own. As one religion
contradicts another, or as any single religion
is often self-contradictory, so it is with
philosophies. Virtually every philosophy
contradicts the majority of other philosophical
views. And it is also true that there is hardly
any philosophy of life that is not contradictory

within itself in one or more areas. Let's consider some of the better-known and commonly practiced philosophies, and you'll see what I mean.

atheism
i'm certain there is no God

Dwight David Eisenhower once defined an atheist as "a guy who watches a Notre Dame–Southern Methodist University football game and doesn't care who wins." In reality, of course, an atheist is one who does not believe in any supernatural being, and often feels no emotional need for such a belief (though some atheists would much prefer to believe in God). If ever one could be called a self-made person, certainly a consistent atheist could be.

If fanatical religion is one extreme, atheism—the dogmatic claim that there is no God—is the other extreme. To assert that there may not be a Supreme Being or that if there is one, He probably cannot be known in a personal way, is one thing; to emphatically say that there is no Supreme Being is something else again. Usually atheists consider themselves scientific. They believe only what they can see, and since they cannot see God, there must not be one. However, one prerequisite in scientific investigation is the attempt to observe firsthand what is being considered. Therefore, for an atheist to dogmatize that there is no God, he should first have been everywhere and observed everything—in all parts of our universe and in all other universes, and beyond—before he can be sure that God does not exist.

Even if he were able to travel extensively throughout all universes and beyond, and he never saw or encountered God; there would still be another obstacle for him to overcome before he could be positive that there is no God: the invisible world. If there is an invisible world then, naturally, he wouldn't be able to see it no matter where he went or how diligently he searched. If that sounds too extreme, consider the following illustration.

Suppose you and I lived 500 years ago. Further suppose that I told you one day that you shouldn't drink the water out of our well anymore because there were tiny, bug-like

creatures swimming around in it. Upon hearing
my warning you went to the well, drew up
some water, poured it into a container, and
looked at it carefully in the sunlight. Slowly you
poured it from the container onto your hand,
and no matter how earnestly you examined it,
you didn't see a single bug-like creature in the
water. You would probably have concluded that
the bug-like creatures were swimming around
in my head!

Well, what would be the problem? It would
simply be that there are so many things that
are only microscopically discerned; and no
matter how diligently you look at water with
the naked eye, you will not be able to see any
microscopic life in it. You need the means to
see—a microscope. We now know that there is
microscopic life, real life that cannot be seen
with the naked eye.

If it is conceivable that there is unseen life
below man's level, isn't it just as conceivable
that there may be unseen life above man's level?
The fact that we do not have the means to see
that life does not mean that it is not there.
And that is exactly the atheist's problem; he is

gambling that there is no God because he has
not and cannot see Him. I believe that's far too
great a gamble to take.

There are so many things that an atheist, if he
is honest, cannot explain or see; yet, he believes
in them. One may *feel* that there probably is
no God, but to insist absolutely that there is
no divine Being anywhere seems foolish and
unnecessary. Atheism is as bad as, if not worse
than, much that goes by the name of religion.
It is as impossible to defend logically and
philosophically as any extreme religious beliefs.
In fact, militant atheism has all the earmarks of
being a fanatical religion in itself. Therefore, to
adopt atheism as one's alternative to religion is
like jumping from the proverbial frying pan into
the fire.

materialism
what you see is what you get

All atheists are materialists, but not all
materialists are necessarily atheists. That is,
if you are an atheist and do not believe in any
Supreme Being, then naturally you believe only

in what you can see. Nevertheless, a man may be a materialist in philosophy or practice and yet feel that there may be some sort of a God somewhere.

Practically speaking, most philosophic materialists would also be atheistic. Many people, including many religious ones, may denounce atheism and materialism as wrong or inadequate philosophies of life, yet they will still live very materialistic lives. They are what you might call *practicing* materialists while denying materialism philosophically. That kind of materialist normally seeks satisfaction in what he can see—in things—only to find that things leave him very dissatisfied, emotionally drained, and spiritually empty.

Defined philosophically, materialism denotes the teaching that there is nothing in the universe but matter and force, and everything else can be deduced from these two things. If atheism is an illogical philosophical extreme, materialism is its first cousin. To say that you believe only in what you can see is neither true nor logical. You cannot see love; you see only its effects. You believe in it, don't you? You

can't see gravity, but you wouldn't get through
a day alive if you didn't believe in it and act
accordingly. It's not true that you believe only in
what you can see or touch. In fact, anyone who
dogmatically insists upon believing only in what
is visible has no room to criticize some of the
illogical and strange beliefs of some religionists,
for he is guilty of the same fault—building upon
a weak, illogical foundation. Such a foundation
simply cannot lead to truth or any kind of
ultimate satisfaction.

Even though living materialistically may give
you a small degree of satisfaction for awhile,
it cannot really satisfy. Perhaps you are a
materialist who has never thought through your
philosophy. It could be true that you, like so
many others, have been living materialistically
without ever realizing the futility of the
outcome of such a life and philosophy. You see,
ignorance is not bliss, especially in a matter this
important. You cannot build a fully satisfying
life upon that which is false. The end result of
doing so has to be a life full of despair, doubts,
and/or regret.

agnosticism
i don't know and i don't think anyone knows

There are basically two kinds of agnostics, the honest, sincere ones and the pseudo-intellectual, insincere ones. I have a great deal of respect for the sincere agnostic, and a great deal of pity for the one who uses his agnosticism to parade before others what he considers to be his intellectualism.

I think David E. Trueblood, a contemporary author and professor of religion, defined the sincere agnostic as well as anyone. He defined him as "the person who admits that he does not know, and is consequently open to learning."[1] On the other hand, Richard Henry Dana defined the insincere agnostic this way: "A man who doesn't know if there is a God or not, doesn't know whether he has a soul or not, doesn't know whether there is a future life or not, doesn't believe that anyone else knows anymore about these matters than he does, and *thinks it a waste of time to try to find out*."[2] There is nothing wrong in not knowing, but there is a great deal wrong and dangerous in feeling it is a waste of time to try to find out what the truth is.

If you have turned to agnosticism as an alternative to religion, let me urge you to cultivate a sincere agnosticism. Don't allow yourself to develop a "know it all" attitude, for then you will slip into the same illogical trap as the atheist—blind dogmatism. If you close your mind to investigation, you close yourself to discovering great truths that may affect your present or future life tremendously. If, on the other hand, you are a sincere agnostic or skeptic, then I'm confident that before you die you'll discover whatever truth can be discovered in this life about the next life.

If you are a sincere skeptic, I've got more to say to you in chapter 3 and following, so keep on reading.

relativism
it is absolutely true that there is nothing absolute

The comment above, of course, gives away what I think is the basic flaw of relativism. The popular teaching of relativism is that there is no absolute truth; everything is relative. But if it were absolutely true that no truth is absolute, then that truth would be absolute! The real truth is that all things are not relative. Many things are, but not all things. Using gravity as our example again, the laws of gravity work just as well where you are as anywhere in the world.

I taught philosophy on the college level for many years, and I have come to the conclusion that most people who hide under the umbrella of relativism do so in order to be able to do what they please without being haunted by feelings of guilt. If you follow the "do your own thing" philosophy of relativism, I hope you do not become an escapist who lives only for the pleasures of the moment and ignores the responsibilities and the realities of life. If you are living in that kind of make-believe world, then you are just as hypocritical as the religious person who aggravates you. Both of you feign concern for the world's condition while actually living for any personal pleasure you can derive. You could excuse your behavior by just thinking, "It's right for me." Anytime we adopt a philosophy or belief simply to cover up what we are already determined to do, we are insincere and hypocritical. As long as we are that way, we

really cannot entertain any hope of finding truth
or lasting satisfaction and peace.

No, I do not think relativism is a good
alternative to religion. In fact, I do not believe
that relativism is a good alternative to anything!
It is a cruel philosophy that leads you to believe
that it's all right to do your own thing since,
after all, truth is not absolute and no one else
can say what's right for you. As a result, others
may be stepped on, ignored, or treated with
disgust if they get in your way.

Let me urge you not to fall into the trap of
relativism—and it is a trap. While it is one of
the more appealing philosophies, it is incapable
of delivering the goods. A life built upon the
foundation of relativism could easily result in
disillusionment, to say nothing of leaving people
around you hurt and embittered.

existentialism
you have to take a leap in the dark

Though existentialism includes many schools
of thought, several general statements can

be made in reference to it. It is, for instance, another philosophy of despair; in fact, it is probably *the* philosophy of despair. While (to its credit) its followers rebel against the computerization of our age and focus on the individual and his choices and experiences, it emphasizes that the individual is trapped in life. We didn't choose to be born, but here we are and one day we must die. Therefore, the only things that are important, according to existentialism, are the experiences we have and the choices we make during our very limited time on earth.

Some existential writers go so far as to say that life *must* be full of anguish and despair. They believe that the only important things are the choices of the will; therefore, every decision, every choice you make, is a monumental event. What if you make a poor choice that throws you into defeat instead of success? The weight of each choice, therefore, brings great agony to the soul. But this agony becomes the glory of the existentialist. Without it, life would have no meaning at all.

Existentialism is also very irrational. It is a protest against objective thinking or reason.

Yet, to be a good existentialist you must think
your way into the philosophical framework of
existentialism. That involves logic; it requires
a certain amount of objective thinking and
reasoning. An existentialist has to think
through questions such as: What is important
in life? How did we get here? Why are we here?
What is life, anyway? Where's it all going to
end? What's my place in the scheme of things?
What can I do to realize fulfillment, or is
personal fulfillment even important?

These are tremendously important questions
that require some degree of thought, not just
snap decisions or choices of the will. Although
existentialists may say there are no known
or demonstrable truths, the truth is that in
becoming an existentialist, a person acts on the
premise that there are known and demonstrable
truths. Therefore, it seems far better to face the
fact of known, demonstrable truths in this life
than to throw that overboard for a philosophy
that is merely "experienced," leading to only
one certainty—death—and urging its followers
to seek constantly the ever elusive existential
experience.

pragmatism
if it works, it's right—so do it

To be pragmatic is to be practical. That's the meaning of the word. Therefore, on the surface it seems that pragmatism is a good, down-to-earth philosophy to follow. After all, most of us want to stay away from mere theory and have something practical working for us, don't we?

There's another side to pragmatism. When pragmatism is at work in the political arena we call it the "doctrine of expediency," and we deplore it. Often it is expediency that gets us involved in wars, allows our government to continue to skyrocket its spending, and persuades nations to sign agreements that they may have no intention of keeping.

Many a young woman has pragmatically won her "prince charming" by giving in to his demands, only to find out that he was even more pragmatic in skipping out when her pregnancy was discovered. That's the ugly side of pragmatism, and it has left many a life a complete wreck.

To be pragmatic is to be practical, but to be

practical is not always the same thing as being sensible or right. A dishonest policeman may need some quick cash, and so it becomes practical to accept a bribe. The fact that he has done the practical thing does not mean he has done the right or sensible thing.

Having pragmatism as your foundation for life involves the same problem inherent in so many philosophies; that is, man becomes the authority determining what is right and what is wrong. What might be practical for you to do might be harmful to someone else; or what might be practical for you for the moment may have lasting results that are disastrous to you and your loved ones. I'm afraid there is too great an element of chance in pragmatism to make it an all-encompassing philosophy of life. Of course, we're all pragmatic in some areas and to some degree, and we probably should be, but that's quite different than making pragmatism one's standard for living.

After all, some actions we condemn in religious people are done for practical reasons. For example, an evangelist who is supported by the gifts of individual Christians "needs" to make a "good showing." In order to "keep those cards and letters coming" he might resort to all kinds of psychological tricks to get results. I know of one evangelist who was so desperate to get people down the aisles that he finally said, "If you love God and hate the devil, come forward." Of course, those who respond to such an invitation are recorded as having "made decisions for Christ." Those fake decisions pad the monthly totals, the supporters are satisfied, and the money keeps flowing in. That's being pragmatic, isn't it? You and I detest it.

Why even consider adopting such a philosophy as the foundation for your own life? It's not adequate to build a life upon.

humanism
i believe in man

As in some other philosophies, there are some good points in humanism, but I believe its weaknesses far outweigh its positive aspects. Jean Paul Sartre, probably the leading spokesman for atheistic existentialism, said that humanism's purpose is "to liberate and help emancipate mankind, with the result that man becomes an absolute for man."[3] In that single definition, Sartre has touched upon the major strength of humanism as well as its primary weakness.

As with atheism, humanism lends itself to creating the self-made man ruling over his self-made society. It's good for man not to want to be shackled by just any tradition or religious dogmatism, and to want to be the real captain and navigator of his life. I would imagine that nearly every man wants to be free in that way. However, as Sartre puts it, the problem is that "man becomes an absolute for man." In rejecting God, the thoroughgoing humanist becomes a god to himself. That is, the humanist decides what is best for himself and the rest of mankind. Humanism argues, according to Charles Frankel, that "the best possibilities of human beings can be achieved only by a combination of informed intelligence and the candid recognition that man must bear the responsibility for whatever standards he adopts."[4]

Suppose my "informed intelligence" tells me that

atheistic Communism is the best philosophy,
and that making the world communistic is the
best thing for mankind. Since anyone who does
not believe in Communism would be considered
opposed to mankind's best interest, it would
be perfectly all right to eliminate such people.
After all, if you have a cow in your herd that's
got a contagious disease you would think
nothing of destroying that one animal in order
to preserve the rest of the cattle. Therefore, if
my humanism is a communistic humanism,
I could very logically justify mass murder,
getting rid of the "sick" human animals that
are spreading contagious propaganda. Even
though I, as a consistent and a feeling humanist
would be concerned for those thus murdered, if
I really thought Communism was the solution
to all human ills, then such killings would still
be tolerated for the sake of the rest of mankind.
"Informed intelligence," then, is hardly a safe
guide for mankind or for the individual.

Of course, the picture I have painted of
communistic humanism is a very drastic one.
However, let's assume that normal humanism
(if we can talk of a norm) in no way resembles
what I have just described. In fact, let's go

one step further and say that humanism as practiced by the majority of humanists would not for a moment tolerate such inhumane practices as I have described. Even if such is the case, where does that leave us?

Possibly the greatest of modern humanists was Ludwig Feuerbach (1804-1872). His writings had a strong influence on such diverse thinkers as George Eliot and Karl Marx. He probably spoke for most humanists when he said, "What man is not, but wills to be or wishes to be, just that and only that, nothing else, is God." He further stated, "To place anything in God, to derive anything *from* God, is nothing more than to withdraw it from the test of reason...without an account *why*... Hence self-delusion...is at the root of all efforts to establish morality...on theology. Where we are in earnest about the right, we need no indictment or support from above."[5]

One of the most respected American humanists of the twentieth century was Charles F. Potter. He defined his own position (which probably is the position of most humanists) as "faith in the supreme value and self-perfectibility of human personality."[6]

If a humanist's goal is the good of man in general and preserving the nobility and value of the individual, if his means of determining what is best for himself and his fellow humans is "the test of reason," then we are again brought back to the dead-end street of the supposed omniscience of mortal man.

Such an approach to determining what is right and true seems inadequate and potentially dangerous for at least two reasons:

First, an individual's knowledge is finite. How can any one person, or even a group, always know what is best for himself, or others? It's just not possible.

Second, we are primarily emotional creatures, not intellectual—as much as we detest admitting it. That means that most, if not all, of our opinions and conclusions are colored by our emotional makeup and our condition at the time we determine what is or is not right.

Humanism, then, still makes man the absolute authority, the last court of appeal. In my book,

man (including this man) is far too fickle to
become God and the final authority for both
myself and the rest of mankind for time and
eternity.

determinism
what will be, will be

A believer in determinism, Baruch Spinoza said
this: "There is no free will in the human mind: it
is moved to this or that volition by some cause,
and that cause has been determined by some
other cause, and so on infinitely."[7] A nonbeliever
in determinism, George Bernard Shaw called
it "Propaganda of a soulless stupidity...
representing man as a dead object driven hither
and thither by his environment, antecedents,
and circumstances."[8] You may, of course, either
believe or not believe in determinism. If you do
believe in it, then you must believe that you were
determined to believe in it; you had no choice in
the matter. If you do not believe in determinism,
then you believe that you have made your own
choice and have chosen not to believe in it.

Some people are attracted to determinism

because it relieves the individual of personal responsibility and accountability for what he does. It becomes the old "the devil made me do it" game all over again; if the devil is not the culprit, some other circumstance or unknown cause will do just as well. Those who cling to determinism as an escape often find themselves bitterly disappointed when they do not reach certain goals or attain specific successes on which they have set their hearts. Their determinism tells them that there is nothing they can do about it; their failures have been determined. That, of course, can quickly lead to a very despondent, trapped feeling. If such a person continues in his deterministic beliefs, he will eventually conclude something like this: "I'm here; I didn't ask to be here, and there's nothing I can do about it or my future." He can also find himself believing in free will in a hurry, too!

Naturally, to a certain extent, determinism is true. That is, you and I did not choose when and where we would be born. That was determined for us by someone else—our parents. I didn't choose to be white, I didn't choose to be born an

American, and I didn't choose to be born with a double harelip and cleft palate; but I was. In that restricted sense, there is determinism; but in a much broader sense, there is freedom. Jawaharlal Nehru, put it this way: "When the cards are dealt and you pick up your hand, that is determinism; there's nothing you can do except to play it out for whatever it may be worth. And the way you play your hand is free will."[9]

As in the other seven philosophies I've discussed, I must conclude that determinism is a poor alternative to religion, even though I see so much wrong with religion.

your own potpourri philosophy
i'll do it my way

Perhaps long before you began reading this book you had already decided that no one religion or philosophy was sufficient for you. Maybe you have already begun to put together your own philosophy. That's why I address this section to a "potpourri philosophy," one that mixes particular elements of various philosophies.

Let's say that you are developing or putting
together your own philosophy. My hat is off to
you. That's no small project. However, before
you go too far, think about this: when you're
all through creating your own philosophy all
you'll have, at the very best, is a well-conceived
human philosophy of life. In other words,
you would be the sole authority on what is
considered important, which standards are
worthy to live by, how your fellow man should
be treated, what should be believed about
God, and whether it is important to give any
thought to or make preparation for the next life.
Of course, the great danger is that since you
are only human and only one out of billions of
people now living (to say nothing of those who
have lived before and those who will live after
you), you may be wrong. Could you possibly
know enough about any subject—let alone all
of life—to really be an authority and to really
know that your philosophy is the last word and
the safest road for you?

Since I probably do not know you, I would not
know your philosophy; but I can safely say
that even if you have the greatest intellect and

the most stable emotional makeup, that is not
sufficient to guarantee you a flawless, infallible,
and safe philosophy.

Although I believe greatly in men being sincere,
sincerity is no substitute for truth. There is
such a thing as being sincerely wrong, and
the danger of a self-made philosophy is that it
might be built by a very sincere person upon
a wrong foundation or premise. When that
happens, the whole structure is doomed. It may
appear to work well for years; it may even give
some degree of satisfaction and a feeling of
worth to your life. But here are a few important
questions you should face: Are you willing
to live the rest of your life—with its limited
satisfactions—by your self-made philosophy?
Will it take you successfully through the hard
times of life—illnesses, financial setbacks, the
disappointments and heartaches when friends
and family fail you? Will it adequately account
for your own personal failings? Will it offer
any kind of final solutions to those failings?
Would you want your own children, parents, or
grandparents to live by your philosophy? Does it
account for how you got here, why you are here,

and who you are? Is it a good enough philosophy
for the rest of the world? And, finally, will it be a
good enough philosophy to die by?

I remember a story that illustrates the
possibility of being sincere, yet sincerely wrong.
A young mother was traveling by train with
her infant baby to join her husband. It was the
dead of winter in the Midwest plains states, and
deep snowdrifts were everywhere. Having been
separated from her husband since before their
baby's birth, naturally the mother was full of
excitement and anticipation. In fact, she was
so eager to see her husband that every time the
conductor walked through the car she would
stop him and ask, "Conductor, is it time yet for
me to get off?" Each time he would assure her
that it wasn't time, but that he would let her
know when it was.

Finally the conductor came through in the
middle of the night, woke the woman, and told
her to get ready because the next stop would be
hers. The young mother got all of her belongings
together, bundled up her little baby, and got off
the train the next time it stopped.

A little later the conductor came through the car, looking for the woman. When he couldn't locate her, he asked the other passengers in the car if they had seen her. One replied, "Why, she got off at the last stop like you told her to."

A look of horror came over the conductor's face. "That wasn't her stop!" he said. "We stopped to remove a frozen cow from the tracks. She got off in the middle of nowhere, and there's nothing we can do about it now until we get to the terminal. Then I can send a rescue team back."

When the search party finally got back to the spot where the dead cow was lying beside the tracks, they also found the mother and her baby—frozen to death.

The conductor was sincere when he told her that the next stop would be hers. He had no way of knowing that they would stop for a dead cow. The mother was sincere; she simply followed the conductor's directions. After all, she was sure he knew what he was talking about. The people sitting around her were sincere as they wished her well, for they had no reason to be alarmed for her safety. Even so, they all were sincerely wrong.

You also may be sincere. You may be sincere throughout your whole life. And yet, when life is over, you may discover that you have been dead wrong. Then it will be too late. And that is the real danger of homemade philosophies. Your own philosophy may be better than what religion has to offer—I don't doubt that for a moment—but it still may not be good enough.

Before staking everything on either your own philosophy or on some other man-made theories, may I suggest that it just might be possible that you have failed to consider one other alternative. Since I would hate for you to go through life overlooking that possibility, I'd like to talk with you about it.

notes

1. D. E. Trueblood, *General Philosophy* (New York: Harper & Row, 1963).

2. Quoted in Eugene E. Brussell, ed., *Quotable Definitions* (Englewood Cliffs, NJ: Prentice Hall, 1970). p. 10. Emphasis added.

3. Jean-Paul Sartre, *Being and Nothingness* (New York Philosophical Library, 1956).

4. Charles Frankel, *The Faith of Reason* (Octagon, 1969).

5. Ludwig Feuerbach, *The Essence of Christianity* (1841), quoted in *God, Man, and the Thinker* by Donald A. Wells (New York: Dell, 1962).

6. Charles F. Potter, *Humanism A New Religion* (New York: Simon & Shuster, 1930), p. 139.

7. Baruch Spinoza, *Ethics, Great Books of the Western World*, Robert Maynard Hutchins, ed. (Chicago: Encyclopedia Britannica, 1952), Vol. 31, p. 445.

8. Quoted in *Quotable Definitions*, Eugene E. Brussell, ed., (Englewood Cliffs, N.J.: Prentice-Hall, 1970), p. 141.

9. *Ibid.*

have i overlooked something?
chapter four

I've written the first three chapters of this book to expose much of religion's sham and hypocrisy, and we saw an abundance of evidence for it, didn't we? But another critic is even harder on religion than I have been; I'm speaking of the Bible.

That may surprise you. However, Jesus never tolerated insincerity in religious leaders. Consider these statements by Jesus concerning the Pharisees, the top echelon religionists of His day, and notice that I've put in brackets the religious games they played then:

> *Then Jesus spoke to the multitudes and to His disciples, saying: "The scribes and the Pharisees sit in Moses' seat* **[the greediness of religion]***: Therefore whatever they tell you to observe, that observe and do, but do not do according to their works; for they say, and do not do* **[the inconsistencies of religion]***. For they bind heavy burdens, hard to bear, and lay them on men's shoulders; but they themselves will not move them with one of their fingers* **[the strictness of religion]***. But all their works they do to be seen by men. They make their phylacteries broad and enlarge the borders of their garments. They love the best places at feasts, the best seats in the synagogues, greetings in the marketplaces, and to be called by men, 'Rabbi, Rabbi.' But woe to you, scribes and Pharisees, hypocrites! For you shut up*

the kingdom of heaven against men; for you neither go in yourselves, nor do you allow those who are entering to go in **[the bigotry of religion]**. *Woe to you, scribes and Pharisees, hypocrites! For you travel land and sea to win one proselyte, and when he is won, you make him twice as much a son of hell as yourselves* **[the fanaticism of religion]**. *Woe to you, blind guides, who say, 'Whoever swears by the temple, it is nothing; but whoever swears by the gold of the temple, he is obliged to perform it'* **[the mystery of religion]**. *Woe to you, scribes and Pharisees, hypocrites! For you pay tithe of mint and anise and cummin, and have neglected the weightier matters of the law: justice and mercy and faith. These you ought to have done, without leaving the others undone* **[the contradictions of religion]**. *Blind guides, who strain out a gnat and swallow a camel! Woe to you, scribes and Pharisees, hypocrites! For you cleanse the outside of the cup and dish, but inside they are full of extortion and self-indulgence. Blind Pharisee, first cleanse the inside of the cup and dish, that the outside of them may be clean also. Woe to you, scribes and Pharisees, hypocrites! For you are like whitewashed tombs which indeed appear beautiful outwardly, but inside are full of dead men's bones and all uncleanness. Even so you also outwardly appear righteous to men, but inside you are full of hypocrisy and lawlessness* **[the hypocrisy of religion]**. *Serpents, brood of vipers! How can you escape the condemnation of hell?*

-Matthew 23:1-7, 23:13, 23:15-16, 23:23-28, 23:33

A pretty strong indictment, isn't it? And it came from the lips of "meek and mild" Jesus!

One more passage will sufficiently show that the Bible itself is as much against man-made religions as you or I could ever be. This time we turn to another loving man, the prophet Jeremiah. He was known as "the weeping prophet" because he was brokenhearted over his people's sins. Here's what he says:

> *Woe to the shepherds who destroy and scatter the sheep of My pasture! says the Lord...For both prophet and priest are profane; yes, in My house I have found their wickedness, says the Lord...Also I have seen a horrible thing in the prophets of Jerusalem: they commit adultery and walk in lies; they also strengthen the hands of evildoers, so that no one turns back from his wickedness...They speak a vision of their own heart, not from the mouth of the Lord* **[the exclusiveness of religion]**...*I have not sent these prophets, yet they ran. I have not spoken to them, yet they prophesied...I have heard what the prophets have said who prophesy lies in My name...Indeed they are prophets of the deceit of their own heart* **[the unreasonableness of religion]**.
> -Jeremiah 23:1, 23:11, 23:14, 23:16b, 23:21, 23:25-26b

By way of contrast, and as an introduction to truly biblical Christianity, it might be helpful at this point to give you my definition of religion: "Any attempt by man to reach God or final bliss, or man's attempts to be what he feels he must be in order to please whatever god he conceives in his own mind."

You may also recall two other statements I made in chapter 1:

> *Ever since I discovered what the Bible is really all about, I've realized that there's a reality that no close-minded person…could ever know or appreciate.*

> *The happiest day of my life was when I lost my "religion" and found something far more lasting and satisfying.*

I'd like to explain what I discovered in the Bible that produces genuine reality, and why that "something" is so much better than mere religion.

All religions, including the Christian "religion" have one common denominator. They all insist that man must do something or be something to be accepted or loved by God. This leads to all kinds of frustrations, contradictions, and hypocritical attitudes. For instance, one church will say that in order to go to heaven you must keep seven sacraments. Another church, with equal dogmatism, will say that what is demanded by God is that you believe in Christ, repent of your sins, confess Christ publicly, be baptized by immersion in water, and obey God's commandments. A third church will tell the world that the way to eternal bliss in God's heaven is by "taking up your cross and following Christ through self-crucifixion," whatever that might mean.

Here's my point. There is absolutely no difference, in essence, between what these three churches are saying. The same could be said of the creeds of many other denominations within Christendom. All are saying virtually the same thing; that is, that man must be good or do certain things or meet certain standards in order to be accepted by God.

Now, here's the shocker. The Bible...the Book that all Christian denominations claim to go by—does not teach any of the above! Go back and read that statement again. Let it sink in.

What does the Bible actually teach about man's salvation? In a nutshell, God wants man to be saved (and to go to heaven) far more than man does. God is not hard to get or difficult to reach, though such an impression is often conveyed. Before man ever demonstrates any love toward God, God has already loved man. A few verses from the Bible should make this abundantly clear.

> *For when we were still without strength, in due time Christ died for the ungodly...But God demonstrates His own love toward us, in that while we were still sinners, Christ died for us.*
>
> *-Romans 5:6, 5:8*

The reference given (Romans 5:6, 5:8) is the book of the Bible (Romans), followed by the chapter (Chapter 5) and the specific verses (6 and 8). I'll put the biblical reference after each quote I use so that you may check it out yourself in your own Bible if you choose.

> *We love Him because He first loved us.*
>
> *-1 John 4:19*

> *For God so loved the world that He gave His only begotten Son, that whoever believes in Him should not perish but have everlasting life.*
>
> *-John 3:16*

From these verses it doesn't sound as if God hates mankind, does it? These are simple, clear, and easy to understand. They really don't need interpreting. They simply need to be believed. Yet, many men—many religious men—agree that God loves the world and that He loves us before we love Him and even that He loves us while we're in our sins. However, having agreed with all that, these same men will often say something like this: "Yes, all of that is true, but ____." They then proceed to "but" the truth of God's love right out of the picture!

I want you to know that God loves you. He loves you just the way you are. What He hates is sin, but He does not hate a man because he is a sinner. He wants you in heaven, and He longs to give you eternal life as His free love gift, with no strings attached. One of the nicest things about God is that He is that way. He has no gimmicks or angles. He's not after anything you may have; He doesn't need any of your possessions. He was doing fine before you came into the picture, and He'll do all right after you're gone. Nevertheless, this does not change His love for you. He loves you infinitely.

The whole reason Jesus Christ came to this earth is because of God's love for you. God is all-loving in the sense that He loves to an infinite degree, but God is not "all" love; He is not "all" anything. He is also holy, righteous, and just—also to an infinite degree. His love cannot negate His holiness, and His righteousness does not make void His love.

Here's the picture: God is absolutely holy. He cannot and will not tolerate any sin at all in His new heaven and earth. This is what He says: "But there shall by no means enter it anything that defiles, or causes an abomination or a lie, but only those who are written in the Lamb's Book of Life" (Revelation 21:27). The same thought is expressed in Psalm 5:4, "For You are not a God who takes pleasure in wickedness, nor shall evil dwell with You."

Even so, while God is so holy that He cannot allow any sin to dwell in His presence, He is so loving that He provided a way for sinful, imperfect man to be able to live with Him forever; and that's the heart of what is called the gospel. If getting to heaven or being forgiven by God depended in any way upon what we did or could do, we would all be totally disqualified. Perfection, not mere human goodness, is required, and none of us can qualify on that score.

Picture someone brought before a judge for committing a crime. The judge is his friend, but he is first of all a judge. As judge, he sentences him to the limit of the law, let's say $300 or 30 days in jail. The man doesn't have the $300, so he walks dejectedly away from the bench to begin serving his time. Just then the judge stands up, removes his judicial robe, comes down from behind his bench, walks up to the bailiff, and pays the fine for him! That's justice, mercy, and love blended in the same human being.

God's love and justice are perfectly blended, too. We deserve to be separated from Him because of our sin, but He offers us what we do not deserve, based on Christ's complete payment for our sins. The Bible puts it this way: "For by grace you have been saved through faith, and that not of yourselves; it is the gift of God, not of works, lest anyone should boast" (Ephesians 2:8-9). What we could never do ourselves, God in

His mercy and lovingkindness has provided. All that we must do—all that we *can* do—is to trust in Jesus Christ (the One who paid our sin debt) as the One who has paid the way for us.

You see, Christ was none other than God Himself in human form. He was the judge of the universe, who came down from His judgment throne to become the humble Savior of the world. That may stagger your imagination, but actually it's very logical. In fact, it's probably the most sensible thing He could have done.

Let me illustrate. Suppose you wanted to communicate with a colony of ants. What would you do? Would you whistle at them as you would a dog? Would you snap your fingers? Or perhaps you would hold out your hand and say, "Here, antie, antie...come get your butter and bread." Any one of those approaches would go right by the ants and they would keep on ignoring you. However, what if you were able to take on ant flesh and got right down where they were? You could wiggle feelers with them and just have a fantastic time communicating. As unreal as it may sound, that would be the most logical and convincing approach to those ants.

Well, we can't do that, but that's virtually what
the God of the universe did when Christ came
to this earth. God describes it this way: "God
was in Christ reconciling the world to Himself,
not imputing [charging] their trespasses to
them...For He [God] made Him [Christ] who
knew no sin to be sin for us, that we might
become the righteousness of God in Him"
(2 Corinthians 5:19, 5:21).

God took on flesh in the person of Jesus Christ,
lived a perfect life here upon earth, and then
voluntarily gave His one infinite life for all of
the finite lives of mankind. The Bible points
out that "the wages [payment] of sin is death
[separation]" (Romans 6:23), but Christ made
that payment for us. The last half of that verse
(the part you never see on the highway signs)
says, "But the *gift* of God is eternal life in Christ
Jesus our Lord" (emphasis added). Just as
the judge in my earlier illustration made the
payment for his friend so that his friend could
live free from that burden, Christ paid for our
sins so that by trusting Him we might be free
from the burden of sin's consequences and have
eternal life. That's the beauty of God's salvation

as contrasted to the confused, complicated, and impossible ways devised by man.

You say there must be more to it than that. What could we add to improve upon it? God, the One who is offended by our sin, is satisfied; our sin, the obstacle between us and God, has been dealt with effectively; and man, the imperfect creature, now has a way of being made fit for heaven. In fact, God Himself could not find a better way of providing our salvation. He even says it in Galatians 3:21: "For if there had been a law [or principle] given which could have given life, truly righteousness would have been by the law." God knew there was no principle or method to ensure our salvation, so He provided the sin payment Himself, in the person of Christ. Those who really believe that Christ did that for them will receive pardon and the free gift of eternal life. Over 150 times in the New Testament alone God says that the one condition for receiving eternal life, or salvation, is faith in Jesus Christ. Here is one of my favorites: "Jesus said, 'Most assuredly, I say to you, he who *believes* in Me *has* everlasting life' " (John 6:47, emphasis added).

This is biblical Christianity. It is not a system
or a tradition or ceremonies or being blindly
loyal to some church creed. Biblical Christianity
is a Person. That Person is none other than
Jesus Himself. He's the One who makes it all
work. He is the Savior, not some church and
not yourself. He's the One who died for our sins,
and He's the One whom God raised from the
dead, proving that sin and death had really been
conquered! He is completely devoid of any sham
or hypocrisy. You can trust Him when you can't
trust anyone else. So, why not do it?

I repeat, what a contrast between real
Christianity, which revolves totally around
Christ and His work on our behalf, and the
human counterfeit, which makes man and his
programs and schemes its center. There's just
no comparison. Christian "religion" is an empty
shell, but God's way of salvation is the most
beautiful thing this world will ever know.

You may be thinking—as many unbelievers
do—that all that I've said in this chapter is nice,
but that I've based everything upon the Bible.
Of course, we all know, don't we, that the Bible
is full of contradictions and fairy tales? Or is it?

Could it be that you've been sold a bill of goods on this point, too? Stay with me a little longer, and we'll find out just what kind of book the Bible really is.

is there a reliable source of truth?
chapter five

Even though I am unimpressed with much that is religious, I do have a very strong belief in the Bible. In fact, I believe the Bible is everything that it claims to be—the very word of God to man. I want to share with you why I believe that, but before I do, let me tell you a true story.

In mid-July 1969, I was conducting meetings in a small northern town in the central part of America. After the meeting one night, a bunch of us went to the home of one of the men of the church. As about 20 of us sat around a large table drinking coffee and having some snacks, some began asking me Bible-related questions. One of the questions concerned what the Bible said about life on other planets. I tried to give as complete an answer as I thought the Bible allowed. No sooner had I finished than a man sitting across from me said something to the effect that God would never allow man to go to the moon. Even as we were sitting at that table, our first astronauts were on their way to the moon. The rest of the conversation went something like this:

"Well, you realize, don't you, that three astronauts are on their way to the moon right now and intend to land on it?"

"Yeah, I know. But they won't make it."

"What if they do?"

"They won't."

"Alright, they won't. But what if they do?"

"They can't."

"Okay, they can't. But what if they do?"

"It's impossible!"

"Okay, it's impossible, but just what if they do?"

"They'll never make it back!"

"What if they do?"

"They won't."

"Alright, they won't. But what if they do?"

"They can't."

"But what if they do?"

"It's impossible!"

"Okay, it's impossible. But what if they do?"

"If God wanted man to go to the moon He would have put him there to start with. He never intended man to be there. It's just not His will."

I then looked at this fine gentleman and said, "You know, you're the kind of person who makes my job difficult. I visit college and high school campuses nearly every year to speak about the Bible, and invariably someone wants to know

why the Bible forbids blood transfusions. Then
there are those who point out how the Bible
is wrong because it teaches that only God can
create life, yet now man can almost do it in
laboratories. Sometimes, too, they may oppose
what I'm saying about the freeness of salvation
by quoting one of the best-known *Bible* verses of
all: 'The Lord helps those who help themselves!' "

You see, the problem is not with what the
Bible actually says, but with what men claim
the Bible says. For instance, none of the above
statements are found in the Bible. God does
not forbid blood transfusions; the Bible does
not teach that only God can or will create life
(see Revelation 13:11-15); and nowhere does
the Bible declare that the Lord helps those who
help themselves. The fact of the matter is that
it teaches just the opposite: the Lord helps those
who are not able to help themselves.

As I share with you some reasons I believe the
Bible is the Word of God, please keep clearly in
mind that I am not defending man's erroneous
theories about what the Bible may or may
not say. I'm interested in upholding what the
Bible, in fact, does say. Just as religious men

have muddied up the Christian message of the gospel, at times they've also tampered with and misrepresented the source of that message, the Bible. You need to be aware that what you have thought the Bible was like and what you thought it taught may not be the truth at all. Seeing for yourself what is actually in the Bible may prove to be a startling discovery.

Here are four very simple and logical reasons I believe the Bible is the Word of God.

complete prophetic accuracy

Notice that I said "complete" prophetic accuracy. By that I simply mean, the Bible is accurate in the fulfillment of its prophecies 100 percent of the time—not 30 percent, not 50 percent, and not even 80 percent. If you think about it, if God really is the author of the Bible it would have to be completely accurate. If it were not, we would have every reason to believe that the Bible is not all that it claims to be.

Of course, it would be a monumental task to discuss every biblical prophecy, but I'd like

to review enough examples to provide a fair
sampling of the Bible's accuracy and reliability.
Let's begin with some **prophecies concerning Christ**.

His birthplace.

*But you, Bethlehem Ephrathah, though you are little
among the thousands of Judah, yet out of you shall
come forth to Me the One to be Ruler in Israel, whose
goings forth are from of old, from everlasting.*

-Micah 5:2

Roughly 700 years before Christ was born, His
birthplace was foretold. Notice that the One who
was going to come out of Bethlehem of Judea
would be "from everlasting"—an eternal Being.
Two Bethlehems existed when the prophecy
was made. Bethlehem of Zebulun was the larger
of the two, and Bethlehem Ephrathah was
what we would call a little country town. God
specified that out of Bethlehem Ephrathah of
Judea the future Ruler of Israel would be born,
yet He would be eternal in nature, preexisting
before His birth. The New Testament fulfillment
of this prophecy is recorded in Matthew 2:5-6;
Luke 2:4, 11, and John 7:42.

The manner of His birth.

> *Therefore the Lord Himself will give you a sign:*
> *Behold, the virgin shall conceive and bear a Son, and*
> *shall call His name Immanuel.*
>
> -Isaiah 7:14

It's important to note that this Son to be conceived
in a virgin and to be called Immanuel would be
a "sign" to Israel. Some have said that the word
virgin in Hebrew (*almah*) means only a young
woman, not a virgin. If that were true, would
that be any kind of "special sign?" Young women
conceive and bear children every day.

Others feel that the fact that His name would
be called Immanuel, which means "God is with
us," would be the sign. I rather doubt that, too,
because when I worked in a bank in Hialeah,
Florida, we had a lot of Cuban accounts,
including quite a few Immanuels. No, the fact
that His name would be Immanuel was not
the sign; the fact that a young woman would
conceive and bear a son was not the sign. The
truth of the matter is that the miraculous sign
of which God was speaking was that a virgin
would conceive and bear a Son, and that Son

would actually be God dwelling among us. The New Testament fulfillment of this prophecy is found in Matthew 1:18-25 and Luke 1:26-35.

The time of His coming.

> *Know therefore and understand, that from the going forth of the command to restore and build Jerusalem until Messiah the Prince, there shall be seven weeks and sixty-two weeks; the street shall be built again, and the wall, even in troublesome times. And after the sixty-two weeks Messiah shall be cut off, but not for Himself; and the people of the prince who is to come shall destroy the city and the sanctuary. The end of it shall be with a flood, and till the end of the war desolations are determined.*
>
> -Daniel 9:25-26

This prophecy was made roughly five hundred years before Christ was actually born. Regardless what is meant by "weeks" in the passage (a great number of reliable scholars think that it refers to years), the truth I want you to see is that the Messiah would be "cut off, but not for himself." And then—after He was cut off (killed)—people would come and destroy the city (Jerusalem) and the sanctuary (the Temple). Whoever the Messiah would be,

He would have to come to earth and die *before* Jerusalem and the Temple were destroyed. To find out when the city and sanctuary were destroyed you'd only have to refer to any good history book of that period. The Roman general Titus destroyed the city and the Temple in A.D. 70.

In fact, in doing so, Titus fulfilled another prophecy spoken by Christ Himself in Matthew 24:1-2: "Then Jesus went out and departed from the temple, and His disciples came to Him to show Him the buildings of the temple. And Jesus said to them, 'Do you not see all these things? Assuredly, I say to you, not one stone shall be left here upon another, that shall not be thrown down.' "

That prophecy was literally fulfilled when Titus sacked and burned the city. As the Temple was burning, the building's gold ornaments began to melt and run down into the mortar between the bricks. Therefore, Titus commanded that the Temple be taken apart brick by brick to salvage as much of the precious gold as possible.

Daniel's prophecy is amazing, not only because it states that the Messiah would be cut off before

Jerusalem and the Temple would be destroyed,
but also because it actually pinpoints the time
when the Messiah would come. If weeks are
understood to mean years, then "from the going
forth of the command to restore and build
Jerusalem until the Messiah the Prince there
shall be seven weeks, and sixty-two weeks"
would mean that from the time the command
was given to restore Jerusalem and its walls
to the time the Messiah would come would be
483 years. The word weeks, in Hebrew, literally
means "sevens." It can refer to a week of days,
a week of weeks, a week of months, or a week
of years. In the prophecy, there are 69 weeks
from the commandment to restore and rebuild
Jerusalem and the walls, or 69 times 7, which
equals 483. If it refers to years, then (using the
Hebrew calendar as our basis) the time between
the command given in Nehemiah 2:1-8 and the
Messiah would be 483 years. That would bring
the fulfillment of the prophecy up to the last
week of Christ's life, the week in which He was
cut off (crucified)!

Even one prophecy as minute as this, written
so far in advance of the actual event, is beyond

the ability of any mere man to create and fulfill. This is just one among many in the Bible.

He would die for the sins of others (not for anything He had done) and be buried in a rich man's tomb.

All we like sheep have gone astray; we have turned, every one, to his own way; and the Lord has laid on Him the iniquity of us all. He was oppressed and He was afflicted, yet He opened not His mouth; He was led as a lamb to the slaughter, and as a sheep before its shearers is silent, so He opened not His mouth. He was taken from prison and from judgment, and who will declare His generation? For He was cut off from the land of the living; for the transgressions of My people He was stricken and they made His grave with the wicked—but with the rich at His death, because He had done no violence, nor was any deceit in His mouth.

-Isaiah 53:6–9

If Jesus were merely a man and had planned to present Himself to the Jews as their Messiah, as a book such as *The Passover Plot* assumes, how could some prophecies be literally fulfilled while He was hanging on the cross or after He had already died? For instance, once He was dead, His body was given by Pilate to a man named

Joseph from Arimathaea, a rich man who laid Christ's body in his own unused tomb (Matthew 27:57-60). If Christ were merely human, He would have had no control over that; yet Isaiah's prophecy was fulfilled to the letter. Christ was buried among the wicked in a rich man's tomb after having paid for the sins of the world.

There is one other prophecy regarding Him over which He would have had no power had He been only a man.

Men would gamble for His cloak while He was being crucified.

> *They divide My garments among them, and for My clothing they cast lots.*
>
> -Psalm 22:18

Try to get the picture. Christ was hanging upon a cross. His hands and feet bleeding from the spikes driven through them, and His head bleeding because of the crown of thorns mockingly jammed down on His forehead. He was exhausted and near the point of death. If He were merely a man hanging there, He would have had very little power at all to even know what was going on, much less to control events around Him. Yet, here is what happened: "Then they crucified Him, and divided His garments, casting lots, that it might be fulfilled which was spoken by the prophet: 'They divided My garments among them, and for My clothing they cast lots' " (Matthew 27:35).

I don't care how well planned a so-called Passover plot might have been; it could not have foreseen this. No, it was not mere chance that had Him crucified; it was not the "fickle finger of fate" that caused the Roman soldiers to gamble for His cloak; and it was not just coincidence that moved Joseph to beg the body of Jesus from Pilate. It was, in fact, the God of the universe fulfilling the prophecies He had given centuries before through His prophets.

In addition to prophecies referring to Christ, there are many **other prophecies** that have also been fulfilled. Perhaps one of the greatest prophetic evidences that the Bible is true is the Jew. Over and over again God foretold that He would scatter the nation Israel throughout the entire world, that they would remain a distinct people during their dispersion, and that one day

He would bring them back again to the land of
Palestine. Here's one of those many prophecies:

> *For the children of Israel shall abide many days*
> *without king or prince, without sacrifice or sacred*
> *pillar, without ephod or teraphim. Afterward the*
> *children of Israel shall return and seek the Lord their*
> *God and David their king and fear the Lord and His*
> *goodness in the latter days.*

-Hosea 3:4-5

The Jewish people have been scattered from
their land for 2,000 years. They have been
without a country to call home, without a king,
without their Temple (which was the center of
their religious life); and yet they have been and
are to this day a separate and distinct people.
They were not assimilated into or swallowed
up by the nations to which they were scattered.
Other than by this one nation, that feat has
never been accomplished in the history of
mankind. No other nation driven from its land
into many other countries has remained distinct
for more than 150 to 200 years. But here is Israel
who has not had her own land—no place to call
home—and yet has maintained her identity, her
customs, and her language for 2,000 years.

Although in 1948 Israel again became an official nation—which was no small miracle in itself—the real miracle is that she was still around to become a nation after 2,000 years! Yet, the greater miracle will still occur in the future when God will take her back miraculously to her land to seek the Lord. Many Jews are going back to Israel today for many different reasons, but when God takes Israel back, it will be just as miraculous as when she left Egypt and crossed over the Red Sea on dry ground. God will do it just as He has kept her distinct all these centuries.

Therefore, 100% accurately fulfilled prophecy is one reason I believe the Bible is true. Let me briefly give you three other reasons.

scientific accuracy

The Bible is not a science book. That is, it was not intended as a book to explain all the mysteries of the universe. However, whenever it touches upon something scientific it is always accurate in regard to facts. It may not always be in agreement with current theories of science,

any more than it has been in agreement with
past theories now known to be false.

Isaiah 40:22 speaks of God as "He who sits
above the circle [literally, the sphericity] of the
earth." This passage, written in approximately
700 B.C., refers to the roundness of the earth;
it says that the earth is spherical, as a ball
is. Isaiah himself did not know that the earth
was round; God revealed it to him and he
wrote it down. In fact, some people today
do not know the earth is round. In the early
days of America's space exploration, one of
the unmanned space vehicles photographed
the earth from outer space. Naturally, the
photographs showed the earth to be round.
However, a group in England known as the
Flat Earth Society would not believe the
photographic evidence. They made a public
statement to the effect that the photographs
were deceptive because, though the earth might
be round, it is only round as a saucer is round.
Otherwise it is flat. They concluded that the
earth is not spherical.

Isaiah wrote nearly three millenniums ago that
the earth is round in a spherical way. How did

He know? The truth, again, is that he did not know; it was revealed to him by God.

Here are a few other striking biblical statements that are now known to be scientifically accurate but were not known to be so at the time they were written: Leviticus 17:11 says, "The life of the flesh is in the blood." Some medical men even call the bloodstream "the river of life." Our bloodstream carries all the benefits of the food we eat to the various parts of our bodies so that the food becomes muscle and tissue. Though men have appreciated the importance of the blood to man's health and well-being, it hasn't always been understood that the body cannot sustain life without blood. However, God, through His Word, told us nearly 3,500 years ago that the life of our flesh actually springs from the blood. In fact, the death of our first president, George Washington, was caused in part by a practice known as "blood-letting."

Washington had been horseback riding for several hours in the cold and snow on December 12, 1799, and when he returned home he was exhausted. The following day he had an attack of acute laryngitis. While being treated with

gargles of molasses, vinegar, and butter, and
a blistered preparation of dried beetles placed
on his throat, he was bled heavily four times.
As a result, his strength and vitality rapidly
declined, and he died at 10pm on December 14.
The medical men of the day practiced what
they thought was very scientific and safe. They
believed that if a person had a fever, the disease
was in his blood. They concluded that if he were
sufficiently bled, the fever or disease would
come out with the blood. Of course, if he didn't
get well soon enough, he would eventually die.
How astounding that the Bible has been so
accurate about this fact all these centuries.

Another interesting statement about blood is
made in the New Testament. Acts 17:25-26 says
that God is not "worshiped with men's hands, as
though He needed anything, since He gives to
all life, breath, and all things. And He *has made
from one blood every nation of men* to dwell on
all the face of the earth, and has determined
their pre-appointed times and the boundaries of
their dwellings" (emphasis added).

I was a very young boy during World War II.
During that period in our history, blood

transfusions and plastic surgery became quite
commonly used, either for saving men's lives
or reconstructing portions of their bodies
so that they could live normal lives. I recall
conversations among my relatives to the effect
that "they'd better not ever try to put any Negro
blood in my boy, or they'll answer to me!" They
believed a black man's blood was inferior to
that of a white man. In fact, upon hearing such
statements, I'd get a determined feeling inside
that if I ever had a son, "they" had better never
try it with him either. It's amazing how far-
fetched our prejudices can be.

Now I'm a little older and, I hope, a little wiser.
I've discovered a few things in my life, and one
of them is that when you go to a blood bank, you
don't order blood this way: "Well now, let's see.
I think today I'll have a little Outer-Mongolian
blood, say about half a pint. Also, let me have
another pint of brown blood with just a drop or
two of red blood. And finish it all off with three-
quarters of a pint of yellow blood." No, blood is
just not cataloged that way. We may have to
specify our blood type, but not from what race
or nationality it comes. But the Word of God
states clearly that He has made "of one blood"

all nations of men. Amazing, isn't it?

I could go on and on listing and elaborating
upon the scientifically accurate statements
found in the Bible. They truly are astounding,
and they give me good reason to believe that
what is recorded in this Book is far beyond
man's grasp, wisdom, or intellectual prowess.
Mere man could not have been the author of the
Bible, even if he had wanted to be.

what it does *not* say

I especially want you to follow the logic of what
I'm about to say, because I consider this to be
the greatest proof that the Bible is of divine
rather than human origin. Of course, the Bible
itself states that God used men in the writing
of Scripture, but it just as clearly points out
that the thoughts and words of the Bible did not
originate with man. The Bible says this about
its origin:

> *Knowing this first, that no prophecy of Scripture is of*
> *any private interpretation, for prophecy never came*
> *by the will of man, but holy men of God spoke as they*
> *were moved [led, or borne along] by the Holy Spirit.*

-2 Peter 1:20-21

The point I'm making is that I believe the Bible
to be the inspired and infallible Word of God
because of what is *not* contained in it. I mean
that God, using specially chosen men, took
roughly 1500 years to have the entire Bible
written. He used approximately 40 human
authors over that period of time. Many of these
men never knew one another; many were not
even contemporaries. They ranged from kings
to shepherds, from lawyers to fishermen, and
from doctors to tax collectors. They came from
all kinds of cultural backgrounds, with varying
degrees of education or lack of education.
Some were national leaders while others were
recognized by few. They wrote about the known
and unknown, and about such far-reaching
subjects as nature and farming to angels and
demons. Yet, when all the writings of these 40
men are brought together, there is not a single
contradiction between them; the 66 books
that make up the Bible form one complete,
harmonious, and organized whole.

Now, follow this. Possibly the oldest book in the
Bible is Job, though earlier events are recorded

in Genesis. Job is the man whom God inspired
to write these words: "He stretches out the
north over empty space; He hangs the earth
on nothing" (Job 26:7). Job is stating two very
amazing things in this verse. First, in the north
there is an empty place that we commonly call
the North Pole, the place that is totally desolate
and devoid of human life and civilization.
Second, he says that God "hangs the earth on
nothing," one of the clearest declarations in
unscientific terms of the earth's existence in
space.

It would have been very easy for Job to have
said something entirely different about this
particular subject, for undoubtedly the educated
men of his day did not believe that the earth
was suspended in space. History records that
ancient Hindus believed that the earth was
on the back of an elephant, that the elephant
was standing on the back of a giant tortoise,
and that the tortoise was swimming in the
cosmic sea. Very scientific, wasn't it? However,
Job didn't follow the "science" of his day. Also,
ancient Egyptians held that the earth was
suspended upon five posts, or pillars. Ancient

Greeks believed the myth that a giant named Atlas was holding the earth on his back. Nevertheless, Job didn't cite any "scientists" or learned men of his day as authorities on this subject.

My point is that if Job and the other biblical writers were simply writing down what they *thought* to be true regarding God and the universe, *they obviously would have written many things thought to have been true in their time, but which would have been proven untrue by succeeding generations.* It would have been humanly and mathematically impossible for a compilation of that many books, by that many human authors, upon as many subjects as the Bible touches, over a 1500 year period, not to include hundreds of false statements believed by those generations, but there is not a single incident of such a statement in Scripture.

I have to conclude one thing: the Mind that moved the men who wrote the Bible was far greater than any human mind or collection of human minds could ever be. In fact, some of the men, like Daniel, admitted that they did not even understand what they were writing

(see Daniel 12:8-9). I believe this has to be the
greatest proof that the Bible is really from God.
After all, 40 men living today couldn't even
write a paper on the best way to grow crab
grass and perfectly agree on it! Why should I
think that 40 men writing on every conceivable
subject, without any contradiction or error,
were writing only from their own initiative and
ability? The very thought is too far-fetched for
my mind to grasp.

it works!

Taken by itself, the fact that the Bible's message
works would not be an adequate reason for
believing the Bible is God's Word. Many
philosophies and religions seem to "work" in the
lives of their followers, so that in itself would
not be proof; but certainly it is true that if the
Bible is the Word of God, it would work and it
does!

The Bible says that once you trust Christ as
your Savior, you become a child of God. As His
child, certain things become true regarding
your relationship to God that were not true

before. For instance, the Bible says, "For whom the Lord loves He chastens, and scourges *every son* whom He receives. But if you are without chastening...then you are...not sons" (Hebrews 12:6, 12:8, emphasis added). God does not treat the unbeliever as He does His own child. Just as any good parent will train and punish a child when and how he needs it, God trains and disciplines those who have trusted in Christ.

I don't think I'll ever forget the first month of my Christian life. Soon after I trusted Christ as my Savior I went to a Christian friend of mine and asked, "Zeke, is there any way to get out of this?"

He asked, "Out of what?"

My reply was, "Out of being saved."

He laughed. Then he asked me why I would want to get out of being saved. When I told him it was because I had never been so miserable in all my life, he really laughed. I wanted to clobber him.

You see, before I knew the Lord, I could do almost anything and get by with it and just simply laugh it off. Yet, once I trusted Christ, it seemed that the least thing I did wrong made me miserable. I could hardly stand it.

Well, my friend explained the truths found in chapter 12 of Hebrews—that God was now my Father and I was His son, and that He would correct or discipline me when and where I needed it. In fact, Scripture made it clear that if I was without chastening from the Lord, it would be a good indication that I didn't belong to Him at all. That was my first lesson of the reality that the Bible is a practical book, and that its truths actually work in everyday life.

In addition to the Lord's chastening, God spells out in His Word many other things that the believer can see working in his life, and by those things he can know that God is true to His Word. The apostle Paul put it this way when he was writing to the Thessalonian Christians:

> *For this reason we also thank God without ceasing, because when you received the word of God which you heard from us, you welcomed it not as the word of men, but as it is in truth, the word of God, which also effectively works in you who believe.*

-1 Thessalonians 2:13

When I say that the Bible is the Word of God and that it proves itself to be just that, I'm not trying to get you to deposit your brains on the shelf and stop thinking. If I were trying to persuade you to believe some fallible church dogma, you might have to take it just by *blind faith*, but God invites men to investigate the claims of His Word. Consider, for instance, these passages from the prophet Isaiah: " 'Come now, and *let us reason together*,' says the Lord, 'Though your sins are like scarlet, they shall be as white as snow; though they are red like crimson, they shall be as wool' " (Isaiah 1:18, emphasis added). Then Isaiah 55:8-9 says, " 'For My thoughts are not your thoughts, nor are your ways My ways,' says the Lord. 'For as the heavens are higher than the earth, so are My ways higher than your ways, and My thoughts than your thoughts.' " God invites us to "reason" with Him. His Word is not contrary to our logic, but because He is its Author it may often be above our logic. That's really as it should be if God wrote it.

Then consider this passage:

I have declared the former things from the beginning;

*they went forth from My mouth, and I caused them to
hear it. Suddenly I did them, and they came to pass.
Because I knew that you were obstinate, and your neck
was an iron sinew, and your brow bronze, even from
the beginning I have declared it to you; before it came
to pass I proclaimed it to you, lest you should say, 'My
idol has done them, and my carved image and my
molded image have commanded them.*

-Isaiah 48:3–5

God understands that we are stubborn and that
we need to be shown. That's the whole purpose
of God prophesying what would happen before it
happened—so that we would know that no mere
man or group of men could have performed what
He did.

I challenge you to face honestly the real
possibility that the Bible may be exactly what
it claims to be—God's revelation to man. Don't
judge God or His Word by men who pretend
to represent Him. There may be a lot of
ecclesiastical garbage in men's opinions, but
there's none at all in God's Word. You can trust
the Bible. Perhaps you may not be able to trust
me or other men or even yourself, but you can
trust the God who is alive and who loves you.

To assist you in determing if the Bible is of
divine origin, here are two lists — one of **fulfilled
prophecies**, and the other of **scientific statements**
recorded in Scripture. I trust you will weigh the
evidence carefully and sincerely.

biblical prophecies and their fulfillments

The virgin birth of Christ.
Isaiah 7:14 fulfilled in Matthew 1:18, 24-25

Messiah to come through Abraham's seed.
Genesis 22:18 fulfilled in
Matthew 1:1 & Galatians 3:16

Messiah to come through the tribe of Judah.
Micah 5:2 & Genesis 49:10 fulfilled in Luke 3:23-33

Messiah to come through the family line of Jesse.
Isaiah 11:1 & 11:10 fulfilled in
Matthew 1:6 & Luke 3:23-32

The birthplace of Christ.
Micah 5:2 fulfilled in Matthew 2:1

Christ's preexistence.
Micah 5:2 fulfilled in John 1:1-3 & Colossians 1:17

Jesus would be Immanuel—God with us.
Isaiah 7:14 fulfilled in
Matthew 1:23, John 1:1-2 & 1:14

Messiah would be preceded by a messenger.
Isaiah 40:3 fulfilled in Matthew 3:1-2

Christ would have a ministry of miracles.
Isaiah 35:5-6 fulfilled in Matthew 9:35

He would enter Jerusalem on a donkey.
Zechariah 9:9 fulfilled in Luke 19:35-37

He would be forsaken by His disciples.
Zechariah 13:7 fulfilled in Mark 14:50

He would be silent before His accusers.
Isaiah 53:7 fulfilled in Matthew 27:12-19

He would be bruised and wounded.
Isaiah 53:5 fulfilled in Matthew 27:26

He would be smitten and spit upon.
Isaiah 50:6 fulfilled in Matthew 26:67

He would be mocked.
Psalm 22:7-8 fulfilled in Matthew 27:31

His hands and feet would be pierced.
Psalm 22:16 fulfilled in Luke 23:33

Messiah would be rejected by His own people.
Isaiah 53:3 fulfilled in John 1:10-11, 7:5 & 7:48

His garments would be divided among the soldiers, and lots would be cast for them.
Psalm 22:18 fulfilled in John 19:23-24

His side would be pierced.
Zechariah 12:10 fulfilled in John 19:34

He would be buried in a rich man's tomb.
Isaiah 53:9 fulfilled in Matthew 27:57-60

scientific truths found in the bible

The earth is spherical.
Isaiah 40:22

There is an empty place in the north.
Job 26:7

The earth is suspended in space.
Job 26:7

There are four "corners" (pivots) of the earth.
Isaiah 11:12

Air has weight.
Job 28:25

The wind travels in currents.
Ecclesiastes 1:6

Light can be parted.
Job 38:24

The body cannot sustain life without blood.
Leviticus 17:11

Not all flesh is the same.
1 Corinthians 15:39

All nations of men are of one blood.
Acts 17:24-26

Every star is different from all other stars.
1 Corinthians 15:41

The stars are numberless.
Jeremiah 33:22

reality at last
chapter six

Lasting reality is not found in religion, in philosophy, in things, or in personal possessions. True reality is found in knowing the Creator and God of the universe in a personal way, and it is possible to know Him that way. I know Him personally, and you can, too.

Try to keep in mind that what I'm talking about is not religion. Remember, religion may be no more than man's attempt at pleasing or reaching God by his own efforts and schemes. God's salvation, on the other hand, is what He has already done to reach man, making the way to heaven possible. True Christianity did not begin with the birth or public ministry of Jesus Christ. It began with the first man, and from then on God repeatedly told His people of a coming Redeemer-Messiah who would pay for and forgive sin. Those who lived before the actual coming of that Messiah were saved by trusting that One, yet unborn. Those who live on this side of His death and resurrection are saved by trusting that same Savior who has already paid for sin.

God wants you to be certain of having eternal life and of going to heaven when you die. Let me share a passage or two from the Bible telling how you may be sure of having eternal life right now.

First, John 3:16, probably the best known verse in the Bible, makes God's way of salvation very clear. It says, "For God so loved the world that He gave His only begotten Son, that whoever believes in Him should not perish but have everlasting life."

Notice that God loves the world. The Greek word translated "world" means "mankind." That would include you, wouldn't it? God so loves everyone—the world—that He did something. That "something" was that He gave His only begotten Son, Jesus Christ. Why did He do that? Here's a passage that tells us why:

> For this is good and acceptable in the sight of God our Savior, who desires all men to be saved and to come to the knowledge of the truth. For there is one God and one Mediator between God and men, the Man Christ Jesus, who gave Himself a ransom for all.
>
> -1 Timothy 2:3-6

The Father sent Christ to die and pay for all our sins—past, present, and future. Having made the payment for our sins, He rose from the dead and is alive today as the living Savior.

John 3:16 goes on to say, "whoever believes in Him [Christ] should not perish, but have everlasting life." God loves the whole world so much that anyone in the world who believes in or trusts in Christ will not perish (be separated from God in a place called hell), but will have eternal life. For you to have eternal life, you must believe in Christ. What does that mean? For one thing, it *does not* mean just to believe certain things about Christ, for example, that He was virgin born, rose from the dead, and will come again. The Greek word translated "believe" literally means "to trust," "to depend upon," or "to rely on." In other words, to believe in Christ is to trust Him to do what He said He would do—give you everlasting life. It is to depend upon or to rely on Him to keep His promise that when you do trust Him to save you or give you eternal life, He'll do just that!

God is eager for you to know that you have eternal life, something that mere religion (Christian or otherwise) cannot offer or guarantee. In fact, He's so desirous that you have this assurance that He has written an entire passage of Scripture just for the purpose of imparting this certainty to you. It's 1 John 5:9-13. Let's look at it one verse at a time. (The emphases are added.)

Verse 9: "If we receive the witness of men, *the witness of God is greater;* for this is the witness of God which He has testified of His Son."

We receive and believe man's witness about things every day. We believe the date on the front page of the daily newspaper; we believe weather reports (sometimes!); and girls and guys believe it when their heartthrobs say, "I love you." Likewise, we should believe God, for He is never wrong and "cannot lie" (Titus 1:2). God does not play little games with us. He doesn't say one thing and mean something else. He isn't a slick salesman who gives you something in large print and takes it away in small print. He says precisely what He means, and He means what He says. He, above everyone else, can certainly be believed.

Verse 10: "He who believes in the Son of God has the witness in himself; *he who does not believe God* *has made Him a liar, because he has not believed* the testimony that God has given of His Son."

If you are already trusting Christ as your Savior, you know it; and if you haven't trusted Him as yet, you know that, too. Nevertheless, when you don't trust in Christ, it's the same thing as saying, "God, You're a no-good, rotten liar. I don't believe You are telling the truth about this eternal life bit!" I'm sure that if God appeared to you in person, you wouldn't shake your fist in His face and call Him a liar. Although, in reality, that's what we do when we do not believe his word to us about eternal life being offered through faith in Christ. This verse clearly states that the reason we make God seem a liar is because we do not believe "the record that God gave of his Son." What is that record?

Verse 11: "And this is the testimony: that God has given us eternal life, and *this life is in His Son.*"

Eternal life, according to the whole testimony of Scripture, is always a free gift. It is not a reward for a good life; it is not something you work for or earn through your effort; it is God's love gift to you when you trust Christ for it. Notice, too, that this eternal life is "in his Son." Eternal life is not in a church or organization. Religion cannot give it to you. Philosophy is powerless to impart it. You cannot give it to yourself. No other man, such as a priest, rabbi, or minister, can present it to you. Eternal life is found only in the Lord Jesus Christ. That's why it is useless to look to religion for it. Buddha cannot give it; it isn't his to give. He said while he was on earth that he didn't even understand this life, much less the next life. Neither does Muhammad have eternal life to give, nor do any religious leaders—living or dead.

Eternal life is the very nature of Christ's life. Remember the prophecy in Micah 5:2 which prophesied the birthplace of Christ? As you recall, that same prophecy said that the One who was to be born was also the One who has "been…from everlasting." The life in Christ is everlasting in nature. His life is immortal while ours is mortal. He lives; we die. It just seems to make sense that if I want to know how to live forever, I'd better listen to the only one who has eternal life to give—the Lord Jesus Christ.

Verse 12: "He who *has* the Son *has* life; he who *does not* have the Son of God *does not have* life."

Only two classes of people are in the world—those who trust in Christ and therefore have eternal life, and those who do not trust in Christ and therefore do not have eternal life. Men, even religious men, may look upon others as rich or poor, black or white, yellow or brown, important or unimportant, powerful or weak; but God does not look upon men that way. With God there is only one issue—how are you related to His Son, Jesus Christ? The issue is not "Are you a member of the First Super-Duper Baptolopian Church?" or "How many Bible verses have you memorized?" or "How many perfect-attendance ribbons do you have for Sunday school?" Nothing like that even enters into the picture. The gut issue is—are you trusting Christ to be your Savior? If you are, or when you do, you have eternal life. It's that simple.

Simplicity is to be highly valued, especially in light of the confusion and supposed depth of many religions and philosophies. I want you to notice that when the greatest Mind in the whole universe—God—put the deepest truth down on paper, He did it all in one-syllable words. Let's read verse 12 again: "He who has the Son has life; he who does not have the Son of God does not have life." That's amazing, isn't it? Everyone can grasp it.

Verse 13: "These things I have written to *you who believe* in the name of the Son of God, that you may *know* that you *have* eternal life, and that you may continue to believe in the name of the Son of God."

The above verse states the two reasons God led John to write his first epistle: (1) so that those who already believe in Christ may have God's assurance that they have eternal life right now; and (2) so that any reader of the epistle who has not yet believed in Christ may do so. I want you to particularly notice that the author, who is God, says you may know that you have eternal life when you trust in Christ. The verse doesn't say that those who depend upon Christ may "think" they have eternal life or "hope" they have it or "guess" they do. It doesn't say that those who trust Christ will have "life until they sin again" or "temporary" life or "probationary" life. No, no, a thousand times no! That's the

accursed gospel of the religionists. God hates
such an uncertain, muddied message.

Read it again: "you who believe in the name
of the Son of God…may know that you have
eternal life." That's fantastic! You can have
everlasting life by simply trusting Christ.

You say, "But how do I do it?"

You trust Him by believing Him. Believe that
He does love you and that when He died on the
cross He died for you as if you were the only
person alive. Believe that He can be depended
upon to keep His promise of eternal life. Then,
when you have trusted Him, everlasting life is
yours. He forgives all of your sin (Colossians
2:13), puts you in His family (John 1:10-12),
begins living in you (John 7:37-39; 1 Corinthians
6:19-20), and you are then His forever (John
6:37-39, 6:47; 10:27-30; Romans 8:35-39).

Perhaps you'd like to pray a simple prayer to
Him—something like this: "Lord, I'm not sure I
understand everything I've read in this book, or
even that I agree with everything I've read. But
if it's true that You love me as I am, and that

Jesus died for me and rose again to prove that my sin is really paid for, then I'd be a fool not to trust in Him. So, the best I know how, I do trust Jesus Christ to give me eternal life right now. Thank You for the gift of salvation. In Jesus' name. Amen."

I want you to know that even if you still have serious questions and doubts about all of this, you can still trust Christ and He will save you. Come to Him as you are with your questions and doubts, with your sins and hang-ups, with your fears about the past and the future; and He will receive you into His family. Then, with His help, you'll be able to grow and to have your questions answered and your fears relieved, and your future will be brighter than it has ever been.

This is where the importance of a good church comes in. There are good churches, despite the fact that some churches still leave much to be desired. What do I mean by a good church? I mean one where the Bible is held up as the only inspired and infallible Word of God, and where the Bible is taught. Unfortunately, some churches make a big noise about believing that

the Bible is God's Word, but do not really teach
it. They might preach out of it, but that's not the
same thing as teaching it. Some pastors make
it a habit to preach just from snatches of verses
in order to drive home the point *they* want to
make, instead of really teaching their people
and letting the Bible make the points God wants
it to make.

If you have trusted Christ and you would like
to begin growing and learning more, find a good
church. Don't be in a hurry. Visit around until
you do find a good one. Notice, I said "a good
one," not "a perfect one". There are no perfect
churches. If there were, then as soon as you or I
would join them they'd no longer be perfect! Even
in a good church you'll find some hypocrites
or bigots or gossips. Don't let that bother you.
Make friends with those who really demonstrate
a love for the Lord and His Word. Associate with
such people as much as you can. Some of their
wisdom and insight will probably rub off.

If you don't have a Bible, buy one. Get a good
one with a quality binding, clear type, and good-
sized margins so that you can jot down notes or
cross references as you study. There are several

excellent study Bibles. Three excellent ones are:
the Ryrie Study Bible, the Scofield Study Bible,
and the Nelson Study Bible.

Try to get involved with believers who study
the Bible a lot, who practice and believe in the
effectiveness of a continual prayer life, who are
actively involved in sharing the gospel with
those around them, and who are above reproach
in their personal lives.

As you become involved in a good local church,
you'll discover two ordinances that Christ
left for His followers during this age—water
baptism and the Lord's Supper, or Communion.
There's nothing mysterious about either one
of them. Baptism is to be done only once,
while Communion is a repeated ordinance.
Water baptism pictures the fact that you have
believed in and are following the Lord Jesus
Christ. It is an outward testimony to the inner
reality of your faith in and obedience to Christ.
Communion, on the other hand, is a means of
remembering that Christ's body was broken and
His blood was shed for you. It is a special time
for believers to focus their attention upon their
crucified and risen Lord.

As you grow and really begin to learn about spiritual things, you'll find that many things that bothered you before don't anymore. You'll discover that many beautiful things in Scripture or things about the Christian life have been perverted by religionists, and you'll have to push aside your preconceived notions about some of them as you let the Bible itself teach you the truth. It will be a very satisfying experience for you, and then you'll probably begin to appreciate how a guy like me can be so sold on the Bible and so opposed to any perversion of it. You will find it true that the more you understand the Bible, the more annoyed you will become with the world's religious jargon. God's Word is clear and simple; man's opinion is confusing and cloudy. I would give my life for the Word of God; I wouldn't give two cents for the usual religious come-on.

One final word — I'm devoting my life to writing and teaching God's Word. A lot of the writing I do is in the form of personal correspondence. I'd love to hear from you. I mean that. I don't mean that I'd like to hear from you only if you agree with this book or if you like what I've said.

I'd like to hear from you regardless of whether you like what I've said or not. I don't think any less of a person because he doesn't agree with me. If you have any questions or objections, or if you've trusted Christ as a result of reading this book, or if you'd just like to write, I'd love to hear from you. I'll do whatever I can to answer any questions you may have. You may reach me in care of the publisher. If you are still bothered by religion, that's all right, but please don't make the mistake of judging God or His Word by religion—don't reject Him. He loves you, remember? And that's not religion, that's reality.